Letters From Life

LETTERS FROM LIFE

BECKY HEMSLEY

Becky Hemsley at Wildmark Publishing

Email enquiries: info@beckyhemsley.com

ISBN PAPERBACK 978-1-915834-13-3
ISBN HARDCOVER 978-1-915834-16-4

For everyone who finds pieces of themselves
in these poems.

This is for you.

May you find joy, hope and above all else,
love.

AUTHOR'S NOTE

Life. What a wild ride.

Often fast. Noisy. Busy.

And sometimes that can be overwhelming. It can feel like we have no control over it. As if we're not the ones in the driving seat but the ones being taken for the ride.

When I was collating all the poems for this book, I realised that this is exactly what I'd written about in one way or another; life.

About the way it can be heavy but also full of joy.

About the way we can hit rock bottom but also reach for the stars.

About the way we are human for sometimes feeling everything and sometimes feeling nothing.

I wrote everything in this collection as a reminder that we're in the driving seat.

A reminder that sometimes the ride might run away from us a little and we might feel lost or scared or out of control.

But we are human, and it's normal to feel those things.
We are also brave.
We are strong.
We are determined.
We are kind.

We might break, but we will also re-build.

We might fall, but we will also rise.

Life is wild, but so are we.

And we should never let our lights be dimmed or our souls be tamed.
Stay wild ♥

Becky x

CONTENTS

IF MY LIFE WAS A SONG

If my life was a song
Then I wonder who'd listen
Who'd fall in love
With the music I'd written?

Who'd sing my notes
At the top of their lungs?
Be moved by the melody
They had just sung?

Who'd hate the chorus –
The words on repeat?
Who'd feel my rhythm
And dance to the beat?

Who'd want to alter
My pitch and my tone?
Who'd only listen
In secret, alone?

If our lives are all songs
Then perhaps we should listen
More closely to what
Other people have written

And we'll hear the pitch
Of their highs and their lows
The change as their music
Gets faster then slows

We'll learn all their words
And we'll know when to sing
And when to be quiet
And not say a thing

We'll know all their rhymes
And repeated refrains
We'll listen to them
And they might do the same

They might learn the lyrics
And chords to our track
And when we sing our song
Then they might sing it back

And right at the moment
They echo our words
We'll realise just how much
We need to be heard

GROWING UP

BABY STEPS

We have to stop thinking that we've failed every time we fall.

When babies are learning to walk, we don't assume they've failed every time they hit the ground. We realise that they are simply not done trying yet.

We praise them for getting up and going again.
Because we realise that it is much easier to fall down than it is to pull yourself back up to standing.

Babies don't stop trying,
no matter how many times they fall.
They don't give up. They get up.
And they continue to believe they can do it.

Sometimes it takes a long time. Sometimes they need to rest.

But they *do* get up.
They find their balance.
And eventually they walk.
Then they run. They skip, they gallop and they leap.

Sometimes we fall and sometimes we need to rest.

But we have not failed.
We are finding our balance.

And we are preparing to run.

Even if we need to take baby steps
at first.

HEALING

Shouting at others does not make our life quieter.

Speaking ill of others does not make people speak well of us.

And hurting others does not heal us.

The way that cutting someone else's flowers
or depriving them of water
or shutting them in the dark
will not make ours grow.

We cannot expect growth if we don't focus on ourselves.

So we have to nurture ourselves.
Be patient with ourselves.
Allow ourselves light.
Feed ourselves.

We are all born to blossom.
But weakening someone else's flower
will not strengthen our roots.

And strong roots mean we bloom.
Strong roots mean growth.

Yes, we are born to blossom.
To grow.

But we've got to heal our roots first.

BLUE

The sky came to school with me yesterday
And he didn't quite know what to do
But the people in charge said 'don't worry' because
They knew he knew how to be blue

And blue was of utmost importance
It was their marker against which to test
So they told him to be at his bluest and he would
Sail over the bar they had set

But it soon became clear very quickly
They had no understanding of skies
Like how blue only follows from orange and yellow
Each day as the sun starts to rise

And they tested him under the twilight
When his blue wasn't brilliant or bright
Cause he knew that his rest was important and so
They saw sky that was blackened by night

And even when he tried to prove himself
With his lightning, his snow and his clouds
They complained of his energy, moaned they were cold
And they told him those things didn't count

So he learned not to show his true colours
All his talents and wonderful things
Yes, he stopped painting sunsets and sprinkling out stars
And stopped playing his songs to the wind

'Cause they all seemed determined to overlook
All the things the sky knew he could do
And they missed all his colours and magic because
They'd been too busy looking for blue

WINGS

I remember [illegible]
Tiny fingers [illegible] toes
Tiny smile [illegible] dimples
And a tiny [illegible] nose

Tiny little [illegible] and feet
And tiny [illegible] hands
Tiny little [illegible]
That I soon [illegible] to understand

And as the [illegible] turned into years
You grew [illegible] grew and grew
You found [illegible] voice and found your feet
And learn[illegible] makes you you

And now it[illegible] a decade
We have [illegible] round the sun
And ten [illegible]ms a lot
But life has [illegible]ely just begun

And yet [illegible] are ready
To stand [illegible] own two feet
To walk [illegible] the future
And disco[illegible]here it leads

So though [illegible]ems a giant step
For one tha[illegible] was small
The world [illegible] your feet
And you m[illegible] explore it all

See it's ha[illegible] me to fathom
How your [illegible]nds have grown
How quick[illegible] life has raced ahead
How fast th[illegible]rs have flown

But I know [illegible] prepared you
To go soar[illegible]ond the sky
And your w[illegible] are almost ready -
It will soon [illegible] time to fly

A NAME

There's a name in these trousers
A name in this shirt
A name in this lunch bag
And one in this skirt

There's a name in this cardigan
One in these shoes
One in this jacket
That they're bound to lose

There's a name in this book
And a name on this tie
A name on their lips
As they're waving goodbye

And maybe today
They're a name on a list
But under the name
They are much more than this

'Cause one day you might
See that name from those shoes
Accepting a new Nobel Prize
In the news

One day you might
Need a doctor or nurse
And recognise them
As the name from that shirt

One day you might
Watch a film or a show
And see a name listed
That you used to know

Yes, there is a name
And another and more
A long list of names
That you've not met before

But there is a person
Who wants you to see,
To hear them and recognise
All they can be

There's a name in this uniform
But please don't forget
It's the name of a person
Who isn't grown yet

And there is no limit
To how far they'll aim
As long as they're shown
They are more than a name

STARTING SMALL

Life can feel a little 'big' sometimes. A little overwhelming. Suffocating.

We can feel as if we have huge bridges to cross
or giant mountains to move.

And sometimes it seems as if it's a bridge too far and a mountain too high.

But just remember...

No one crosses a bridge without first taking a few steps.
And no one moves a mountain without first moving a few rocks.

Every big job is made up of lots of smaller ones.

Start small.

Small voices can make big change if they don't give up.
Small footsteps can walk long journeys if they keep going.
And small bricks can build huge towers if there are enough of them.

So start small.
And one day - without realising - you might find that
you're halfway across the bridge
or that you've moved half the mountain.

And you might find that life has become a little 'smaller'. A little less overwhelming.

And you'll be able to stand on that bridge for a moment.
Stand with the mountain for a minute.

And you'll be able to breathe.

TRUST

A seed does not worry about whether or not it will grow,
petals do not worry about falling,
and leaves do not worry about wilting.

Flowers do not worry that they will not bloom.

They simply trust.

Trust that there is no rush to grow.
Trust that they don't need to hang on for any longer than is necessary.
And trust that they do not need to look bright and beautiful all of the time.

Because they more than trust - they know –
that they will grow
and they will blossom
and they will come back stronger
once their winter is over.

And so, my darling,
will you.

EXT[illegible]AORDINARY

You are no[illegible] to be ordinary.

I know wha[illegible]'re thinking. You're thinking "but what's so extraordina[illegible]out me?"

Well...

You are so [illegible]rdinary that the moon has to move oceans just to erase your footpr[illegible] from the beach.

You are so [illegible]rtant that the earth itself pulls you close to stop you from floatin[illegible]way.

You are so [illegible] of wonder that your eyes contain more atoms than there are stars in [illegible]nown universe.

And if you [illegible] of all the people you love the most, you will realise that the way in [illegible] you love them is not in the least bit ordinary. You love with such p[illegible] such passion and such fire that it is comparable only to the sun.

No, you are [illegible]ere to be an ordinary thing in an ordinary world my darling.

The world i[illegible] knows you are not.

It knows yo[illegible] magic.

MAGAZINES

"I don't look like the women in the magazines."

Oh, but you're not supposed to. They are a two-dimensional snapshot in time. A work of art on the page that has been practised and posed and styled and edited over and over again.

Your hair is not supposed to look like theirs because it moves with you. It bounces with every step you take; it tickles your child's shoulder as you kiss them goodnight and it curls upon your pillow as you dream.

Your skin is not supposed to look like theirs because it has lived every day of your life with you. It has laughed until it's lined and cried until it's creased.

Your clothes are not supposed to look like theirs because they are along for the ride with you. They are walking the dog and holding meetings and having brunch with friends.

You are not supposed to look like the people in the magazines because you are a living, breathing work of art.

And wouldn't it be a shame if a two-dimensional image stopped you living? If you took all of the angles and facets of what makes you you, and wished they were smoother or softer, silent and still. If you sanded them down until they were indistinguishable. Until you were no longer you.

Because surely living is what we are here to do. In all its messy hair and crumpled clothes and wrinkled skin glory.

A picture can't hug a friend or walk the dog or laugh until it cries.

A picture can't dream.

So it isn't that you don't look like the women in the magazines my darling. It's that they don't look like you.

And you know what?

Maybe they wish they did.

BEAUTIFUL

You are no[illegible]ody
You're a so[illegible]ithin a skin
And that w[illegible] makes you beautiful
Is that whi[illegible] within

So if the wo[illegible]you spoke
Became ta[illegible] across your chest
Or sewn ac[illegible] t-shirt
That you w[illegible]ch time you dressed

If all the de[illegible]ou did each day
Were braid[illegible]hrough your hair
And every s[illegible] that you took
Laid all you[illegible]ons bare

If what's in[illegible]our heart
Was truly w[illegible]n on your sleeve
And your e[illegible]ally were a window
To what lie[illegible]eath

Then could[illegible]ook at what you did
And all the[illegible]s you said
And still m[illegible]n your beauty
With your i[illegible] self instead?

Yes, could[illegible]uly say
Your beaut[illegible]ore than just skin deep
If you look[illegible]our reflection
And it show[illegible]hat lies beneath?

SOS

She cries all her tears to her pillow
And they fall in great dashes and dots
Like a message she secretly whispers
To a world where she's found herself lost

Often, she cries to a rhythm
Like the rain as it falls to a beat
And her tears dance their way to her pillow
As the rhythm then lulls her to sleep

But he has been paying attention
And he's heard every tear that has dropped
So he's reaching a hand out to hold her
And collecting her tears 'til they've stopped

And he does it without expectation
Just as long as she knows he is there
So that if she decides that she'll cry in the light
She can trust that there's someone who cares

You see, when the night is upon us
And we simply can't see any more
Well then, all other senses are heightened
And we hear things we didn't before

And she has been crying in darkness
In a bid to conceal how she's felt
But she doesn't know he has learnt Morse Code
So he knows she is crying for help

PENNY FOR YOUR THOUGHTS

One day at [illegible] I met a girl
As I went [illegible] walk
She didn't [illegible] me at first
'Cause she [illegible] in thought

I held a coin [illegible] her
And then [illegible] I said
"A penny [illegible] thoughts"
But she [illegible] and shook her head

"A penny [illegible] be enough"
She whisper[illegible] a sigh
"I think I'd [illegible] hundred coins
To say what [illegible] my mind"

"Well mayb[illegible] with one," I said
And she too[illegible] her palm
She took th[illegible]est breath
And then [illegible]y took my arm

She slowly [illegible] speaking
And her eye[illegible] slightly brighter
Her face [illegible] little
And the air [illegible] felt lighter

I held anoth[illegible]nny out
She took th[illegible] as well
And her bre[illegible] steadied as she
Spoke the [illegible] had to tell

And all of [illegible]tinued
For an hour [illegible] longer
And all the [illegible] her voice
Was growin[illegible]ident and stronger

And then [illegible]hed the wishing well:
She looked [illegible] and grinned
And one by [illegible] wished on pennies
As she thre[illegible] in

Then she told me "thank you"
Waved goodbye and walked away
And I saw her only once more
After seeing her that day

I saw her trading thoughts again
For pennies made for wishing
But this time someone else spoke
For the pennies she was giving

JUST A PHASE

When you look up to the moon tonight, you may only see a small crescent of it.

The shape a child draws when they add the moon to their pictures and paintings.

You will look up and see only a tiny part of the moon,
but you will not think less of it.

You won't think that it is not trying hard enough.
You won't assume it is being lazy.
You won't find it any less beautiful.

You will know that it is simply going through a phase and that one day soon it will be full again.

Well, sometimes we are like the moon.

Sometimes we go through phases where we are full.
And sometimes we go through phases where we can only give others a tiny part of us.

And if that's you right now, remember...

You are not being lazy.
You are still beautiful.
You are enough.

This is just a phase you're going through,
that's all.

Just a phase.

THE GAME OF LIFE

It's ok if you don't know what you want to 'do with your life' at fifteen you know. It's ok to not map your whole life out ahead of you before you know who you really are.

How could a fifteen-year-old you possibly know what life has in store? How you're going to change? The people you're going to meet and the places you're going to go?

It's ok to not map your life out. Period.

Because life is not a game of chess. You don't have to be constantly thinking ten steps ahead. The game is going to end at some point whether you planned it all out or not.

And when the game of life is over, the winner is not the one standing depleted on the board.

We are not here to work until we die.
We are here to live until we die.

And that doesn't mean going on the grandest of adventures each and every day but neither does it mean forgetting that life itself is adventure enough.

So when people ask you what you want to do with your life,
it is enough to say "live it and love it."
And that will look different at fifteen and twenty-five and forty-five and even ninety-five.

If you're always looking ten steps ahead, you're missing out on what's happening right now. On life at this moment.

So work hard, yes. But only to live hard.

Have a sense of purpose and direction, yes.
Use it to steer you right now and then see where it takes you.

Be ambitious, yes. But know that it's ok for some goals to be temporary.

Life is not a game of chess.

You don't have to limit yourself to specific spaces in the world. Specific directions. Specific paths. Specific encounters.

You're here to explore the whole board.
To live it.
And love it.

JULY

One time I met a girl
Who was a burning ball of light
She glowed with endless energy
From morning through 'til night

Her skin glittered with freckles
And her hair was plaited gold
And I decided I would like to be
Like her when I grew old

For every room she entered
Soon became a little brighter
And you'd be warmed right to the soul
By standing close beside her

She made it feel like summer
Even when the sky looked bleak
And she could thaw your winter
With a kiss upon your cheek

And people asked why I would want
To follow in her glow
And I was always stunned
That they just didn't seem to know

'Cause why would I be winter
When I could be warm July?
What a gift to be the sunshine
In another person's sky

CRUMBS

Promise me [illegible]mething...

Promise me [illegible] you'll never let anyone deprive you of the very basics of humanity.

Never let [illegible] make you so hungry that you will accept just
scraps of l[illegible]
crumbs of r[illegible]ect
and tiny m[illegible]ls of kindness

People who [illegible] starving will eat anything. But that doesn't mean they should have [illegible]

You are de[illegible]ing of so much more.

A banquet [illegible]ve
a whole fea[illegible]f respect
and a full sp[illegible] of kindness.

So promise [illegible]ou won't go hungry. And if anyone tries to deprive you, remember [illegible]

We should [illegible]ve enough self-love, self-respect and self-kindness to share.

So if they t[illegible] starve you...

It's because [illegible] are hungry themselves.

LETTING GO

There will be some people in life who just won't be able to love you the way you need them to.
The way you love them.

There will be some people in life who won't treat you the way you deserve to be treated.
The way you treat them.

And there will people in life who just can't give you what you want.

Sometimes we cling on to these people for far longer than we should. Like a tree clinging desperately to its leaves, trying not to let them fall.

But they will fall.
Eventually.
And the tree shouldn't blame itself.

Because the loss - whilst great - is necessary. The tree needs to lose its leaves so it can rediscover its roots and ready itself for a fresh start.

You can't keep painting autumn leaves green and expecting them to stay.

Deep down they are always destined to fall.

The key is knowing when to let go.

HISTORY BOOKS

The history books will tell you about the kings and the queens and the conquerors.

They will tell you of the battles they fought and the castles they built; of the voyages they took, the things they discovered and the progress they made.

But the history books won't tell you of the man who joined the fight. The man who left behind a beloved family to help the king win the battle.

The books won't tell you of the girl who dressed the queen each morning or the boy who tended the horses that pulled the royal carriage.

The history books will not tell you of the times the conquerors wanted to give up or give in.

They will not tell you of the person who told them to keep going, who reminded them of their worth; who held them up when they struggled to stand and gave them strength when they felt weak.

So the pages of the history books may tell you that the leaders of the past were made of pure strength, determination and spirit. But do not forget that they had whole armies behind them and whole councils beside them.

Yes, even the queens and the conquerors and the kings didn't go to battle alone. They didn't fight alone, didn't walk alone, didn't thrive alone.

And you don't have to either.

RUBBLE

When life is throwing bricks
And when it's firing its shots
When every day feels like a war
You've well and truly lost

When you have no idea why life's
Determined to attack
And leave you in the ruins
With no obvious way back

Then gather all your strength
And all the rubble at your feet
And build yourself a place
Of rest, resilience and retreat

Build the strongest battlements
Construct the thickest walls
Build the safest keep
And stack the towers extra tall

And you will have a castle
With its turrets and its columns
That you'll have built against the odds
When life had hit rock bottom

Your castle will remind you
That you're tougher than you know
And it will help you realise
That no matter what life throws

You will always have the power
And you'll always find the strength
To use the things it's throwing
To build yourself back up again

QUEEN

They try to [illegible] you down
But what th[illegible] have overlooked
Is that we c[illegible]get to talk things down
If they are l[illegible]er up

They talk b[illegible]d your back
But don't b[illegible]rt by things they've said
'Cause the r[illegible]n they're behind you
Is because y[illegible] way ahead

They talk o[illegible] in whispers
But they co[illegible]ict their point
'Cause they[illegible]oving they're not confident
To speak al[illegible] your voice

See they've [illegible]nced themselves
That you're [illegible] villain in their story
But that's b[illegible]use you shine a light
On all their [illegible] glories

So just igno[illegible] the whispers
And don't g[illegible] backwards glance
Believe you [illegible]ore than worthy
Of your cur[illegible] circumstance

And rise on [illegible]bove it
Draw your [illegible]ders back, stand tall
And keep y[illegible] head held high Queen
Else your cr[illegible]n is going to fall

AT THE MOVIES

I cannot stress this enough: you've got to learn to fall in love with yourself. To romance yourself the way you deserve.

Leave yourself little notes around the house to remind you that you are kind and thoughtful and brilliant.

Take yourself for coffee and get lost in your favourite book or your favourite music.

Cook yourself a three-course meal.
Dress in clothes that make you feel good.

Buy yourself flowers and take yourself to the movies.

Stop waiting for other people to love you. There is no one you deserve to be loved by more than yourself.

So do it.

Walk down the street like there's a soundtrack playing.
Like you are the lead in the movie of your life.

Because here's the thing...

You actually are.
You are the main character.

This is your story. Your movie.

And it will save so much time and so much heartache
if you learn to love yourself sooner rather than later.

Because when your credits roll,
you deserve to have been told you're brilliant.
You deserve to have been made to feel good.

But more than anything else,
you deserve to have been
loved.

SPARKS

There will [illegible] times in your life when your light is too bright for others.

And there [illegible] be times when their light is too bright for you.

And let me [illegible] honest about something...
It is never [illegible]ght's fault.

We always [illegible]nt it to be. We want to blame them for burning so brightly
and leaving [illegible] the shadows. We'll want to extinguish their flame so
that ours ca[illegible] grow.

But all that [illegible]ll mean is that there is less light in the world.

And this w[illegible] needs as much light as it can get. It needs
the lightbul[illegible] moments and
the flames [illegible]ssion and
the sparks [illegible]ope.

You do not [illegible] to stand in the shadows, willing others into them too.

We are not [illegible] to share darkness. We are here to spread light.

So go ahead[illegible]

Shine.

THE GREATEST LOVE OF ALL

If you asked your nearest and dearest what they loved most about you, I bet you'd be surprised at their answers.

Because whilst you're worrying about not being smart enough or pretty enough or generous enough...

Whilst you're wishing you could look better, do better, be better...

They are admiring the way you can warm a room just by walking into it. How you somehow bring light to whatever you do.

They are remembering every time you've been there when they needed you. How you selflessly put them first.

They are smiling as they think of the way your eyes brighten and widen when you laugh. And how you have a way of making everyone else smile and laugh with you.

They are thinking of all the things that make you lovable. That make you, you.

So stop searching for reasons not to love yourself.

You do not need to look better or do better.

You are warm.
You are kind.
You are fun.

You are you.

Maybe it's time to start
falling in love
with yourself.

GRE[illegible]TEST FEARS

“What’s you[illegible]eatest fear?” they ask
We answer [illegible] way
But what we [illegible]eally scared of
Isn’t what w[illegible]ually say

‘Cause we’re [illegible] scared of flying
But of fallin[illegible] the sky
And we’re a[illegible] of failing
But we say w[illegible] scared to try

It’s not that [illegible] afraid to want
But that we’[illegible]red to lose
And we are [illegible]raid to ask
But scared w[illegible] refused

We’re not a[illegible]f water
We’re just s[illegible] that we could drown
And we avoi[illegible] climb
In case we p[illegible]et to the ground

We’re not a[illegible]f caves
But of the t[illegible]hat lurk inside
And it is no[illegible]ark we fear;
It’s the mon[illegible]hat it hides

But if we’re [illegible] of trying
Then we’ll n[illegible]now success
And if we’re [illegible] to hear a ‘no’
We’ll never [illegible] ‘yes’

If we’re terr[illegible]o lose
We’ll likely [illegible] win
And if we’re [illegible] of drowning
Then we’ll n[illegible]earn to swim

So take the deepest breath
And show the monsters you are brave
And maybe you’ll find treasure
In the darkness of the cave

Take the biggest step
And climb the mountain to its peak
Stretch your arms out sideways
And then take the biggest leap

‘Cause, we’re not scared of anything
Except of getting hurt
But life without a little risk
Is not what we deserve

And we can’t miss out on living
‘Cause we’re all too scared to die
For if we’re afraid to fall too hard
We’ll never learn to fly

SUGAR AND SPICE

Sugar and spice and everything nice
That's what they say girls are made of
Sweetness and grace and a beautiful face
Is how they are taught to aspire

But she's bit-by-bit, built intelligence, wit,
Power and strength, irrepressible grit
And if you're nice, she's nice
But you burn her?

And she'll start a fire

LIK[illegible] A GIRL

She drives j[illegible]e a girl you know
And throws [illegible] like one too
She fights j[illegible]e a girl as well
She's just [illegible]ch for you

She also ru[illegible] like a girl
And that's [illegible]y she plays
But when t[illegible] "just like a girl"
I think the[illegible]n to say

Worse
And someh[illegible]less
Somehow [illegible], somehow weaker
They think [illegible] she's 'like a girl'
They'll easil[illegible]eat her

But girls wi[illegible] battle
When they [illegible]dy are bleeding
And girls ar[illegible] at throwing themselves
Upwards th[illegible] glass ceilings

Girls are bu[illegible]igating progress,
Driving cha[illegible]
And girls ar[illegible] winning
Whilst you [illegible]ise their game

So tell her [illegible]e's 'like a girl' -
She may jus[illegible] you right
She may ou[illegible], out-last you,
Win the ra[illegible] win the fight

'Cause she's [illegible]ving force
Fighting fo[illegible]lace in this world
And if you [illegible] talk her down
She'll rise u[illegible]

Like a girl

REAL

I've cried when I'm happy
And cried when I'm sad
I've smiled through the good times
And smiled through the bad

I've screamed in excitement
I've screamed out in pain
I've gasped at the sunshine
And gasped at the rain

I've laughed when I'm nervous
And when I'm elated
I've sighed with contentment
And when I'm deflated

I've sung when I'm lonely
And sung in a crowd
I've shouted when angry
And when I've been proud

'Cause whether we're up
Or we're riding a low
Our feelings are desperate
For somewhere to go

We can't keep them trapped
And locked up in a cage -
They force their way out
'Cause they need to escape

And sometimes we're told
That emotions are weakness
That feeling is flawed
If we let it defeat us

But how can this be?
Surely this must be wrong
For what could be weak
About something so strong

That it cannot be silenced
Cannot be tamed
Can't be kept down
And cannot be contained?

So when you next shout
Or you laugh or you cry
You scream or you smile
Or let out a sigh

Whatever the reason
Just let yourself feel
We're not here to be quiet -
We're here to be real

TRU[illegible] COLOURS

I looked up [illegible] word 'yellow' the other day.

I found so [illegible] shades of yellow that they had been distinguished by
words like
gold
honey
daffodil.

I found wo[illegible] like fire and sand and champagne and lemon and sunbeam
and I even [illegible] a song.

Now imagi[illegible] neone telling yellow that it's 'just yellow'.

When yello[illegible] a sunbeam and a daffodil and fire.
When yello[illegible] a song.

Without yo[illegible], we couldn't make orange and we couldn't create green
and our wo[illegible]uld be far less colourful because of it.

Yellow's tr[illegible]olours are not limited to one thing.
And neithe[illegible]ours.

Some days [illegible]e dark and fiery and intense.

Some days [illegible]e rich and bright and vibrant.

Some days [illegible]e buttercups and dandelions and some days you are
champagne [illegible] song.

And withou[illegible], someone's life would be far less bright and far less
beautiful.

You are you [illegible]
yellow is ye[illegible].

And the wo[illegible]eds you.

Because, no [illegible]er what you think, you are not 'just you'.

You are so [illegible] more.

FRIENDSHIP

Friendship is the type of love that chooses you.

It is a love that chooses you when there is nothing to make it stay.

A love that says
"I have seen you at your highest,
I have seen you at your lowest and I will persevere.
Not because I feel obligated to or because we signed a contract, but simply because you are you. Because you matter to me."

Friendship is the kind of love that doesn't need a lot of grand gestures but it's the kind that chooses to make small gestures that mean a lot.

It drives out of its way to drop off treats at your door when you're not feeling well.
It sends surprise notes in the mail to say "I'm thinking of you."
It sends messages without needing a reply when you're going through a tough time. Because it knows that you might not have the energy to respond. But it wants you to know that it's there.

Yes, friendship is the kind of love that chooses to exist.

The kind of love that chooses you for no other reason than the fact that you are you.

And that's why
it is so incredibly special.

WHEN YOU MEET AGAIN

There are going to be times in life when death steals the people that you love from you. When grief swoops in and descends hungrily and heavily and leaves you feeling empty.

And at those times, it can be hard to get out of bed and open the curtains; to let the light in.

It can be hard to leave the house and speak to people; to let the world in.

It can be hard to know how to go on living when the person you love could not. Hard to see the point in moving forward without them by your side.

But there is one certainty in life.
And that is death.

And one day death will steal you too.

And when that time comes,
wouldn't it be wonderful to be able to regale your loved ones with tales of the adventures you were able to keep having?

Wouldn't it be wonderful to tell them how you took them with you in your heart and how you felt them by your side every step of the way?

Yes.

Wouldn't it be wonderful to live a life that is so full,
that you simply cannot wait to tell them about it
when you meet again?

WHEN

When did we all lose the thrill
Of running full-speed down a hill
Of marvelling at daffodils
Until the sun went down?

When did we stop spending days
On grassy verges weaving braids
Of plaited, fragile daisy chains
Until we'd made a crown?

When did we begin to lose
The urge to skip and race and move
'Til we had scuffed our favourite shoes
All in the name of fun?

When was it that we forgot
Predicting 'loves me, loves me not'
With flowers from a wild plot
That grew beneath the sun?

And when did we begin to miss
The chance to stop and make a wish
With dandelions clocks we'd picked
That grew beneath our feet?

Well I for one do not believe
That we forgot how all that feels
But life at some point took the wheel
And freedom took back seat

It seems that it got left behind
And buried 'neath the daily grind
But it's still there for us to find
At any time we want

So climb a hill then run back down
Weave yourself a daisy crown
Then blow your wishes to the clouds
Because life's too short to stop

TORN

For a long time I would tear myself to pieces trying to play the characters that other people needed on their pages and in their stories.

I would try to remember the lines I thought they needed me to speak and the plots they wanted me to follow.

And so I became a collage of characters. Tiny scraps of different people all a little frayed at the edges.

And sometimes I would do great things and sometimes I would make mistakes.

So sometimes I became the hero
and sometimes I became the villain.
No matter how unintentional.

But that's ok.
I've realised that it's ok.

Because I've since learned that I'm not a character in someone else's story and I don't need to tear myself apart trying to fit in.

I am my own person.
I have my own pages. My own story.

And instead of becoming a collage of who I thought I needed to be,
I've realised all along...

that I only ever needed to be myself.

GROWN

THE [illegible]UTURE

Here lies th [illegible]ure ahead, take a look
A new year [illegible]sh as a never-read book

Familiar ch[illegible]ers, those you've not met
Pages and [illegible]s you haven't turned yet

Chapters sa[illegible]rding hellos and goodbyes
Cliff-hange[illegible] plot twists, the lows and the highs

A world th[illegible]aiting, adventure that's pending
A tale full o[illegible] from beginning to ending

But here is [illegible]et; you're holding the pen
So write in [illegible] interest again and again

See, you ca[illegible]de what your story's about
Write certa[illegible]ngs in and write other things out

And thoug[illegible]re'll be plot twists and painful goodbyes
Chapters a[illegible]ges that might make you cry

You'll ride [illegible]the lows maybe soar from the cliff
Just remem[illegible]our story is meant to be lived

Yes, a neve[illegible] book is just like a new year
Take a look [illegible] ahead
'cause the fi[illegible] lies here

OUTGROWN

Just as a plant must be re-potted,
A baby must move from their crib
And it's time to drain the pan
When water's bubbling to the lid

So too we have to realise
There are times that we'll have grown
And we do not have to stay
If home no longer feels like home

STARGAZING

“How woul [illegible] ou define,” he asked
“What bea [illegible] means to you?
Could you [illegible] into words
So I could s [illegible] too?”

She paused [illegible] st a moment
As she look [illegible] to the sky
“For me,” sl [illegible] aid “true beauty
Lies beyond [illegible] naked eye

You see, fo [illegible] he stars
Are tiny do [illegible] inst the dark
And even cl [illegible] ogether
They’re a m [illegible] miles apart

But even in [illegible] solitude
Or when we [illegible] k they’re small
It doesn’t c [illegible] the way they feel
About them [illegible] s at all

They know [illegible] worth is not defined
By only wh [illegible] see
And so they [illegible] on burning
Taking all t [illegible] pace they need

To me it’s l [illegible] hey’re glitter
Someone’s [illegible] led in the sky
Like tiny lit [illegible] eworks
Reflected i [illegible] yes

For I believe that beauty
Is the fire deep within
That burns until our inner shine
Becomes our outer skin”

And then she turned the question round
And asked if he agreed
But she didn’t turn to face him -
If she had then she’d have seen

The way his eyes were shining
And reflecting fireworks
Because whilst she sat stargazing
He was sat gazing at her

NORTH STAR

I see you, you know – giving out so much light.

You spend your days lighting the way for others, brightening their days and bringing light to their darkness. You are the North Star in their night sky.

But that which gives out light must burn.

And you are burning out.

Your spark has dimmed and your fire is dying. Your flames are small and your energy low.

Your star is fading.

You are giving so much light to others and forgetting to save some for yourself.

But light-givers need light too. They need to collect it, nurture it, treasure it. You can't give out something you don't have.

No, you are not fading, and you are not small. You are tired and depleted. So rest my dear.

Don't let yourself burn out.

Find your light.

TUNNEL VISION

There is so much we miss every day. So much that passes us by, that we barely even see, let alone notice.

The leaf in the shape of a heart. The cloud in the shape of a dragon. The toddler dancing to the busker's music. The man humming show tunes as he shops for milk. The puppy carrying a huge stick in the park.

Little things that make us smile. That we capture with one click of our memory and sometimes with the click of our camera.

Things that we share with the people we love when we get home and say, "guess what I saw today."

But we don't do it enough. We are tunnel visioned, living always a few steps ahead, thinking that we're closer to some elusive light at the end of the tunnel.

But the little stuff is the light - the things that slowly light us up from within, that romanticise our everyday lives. That remind us there is joy everywhere if we look for it.

We can't always rely on the big stuff – the holidays, the parties, the birthdays, the weekends – to fill us up with joy. They are too short-lived, too fleeting.

We need to slowly drip-feed joy into our lives. Our veins. Our souls. That's how we'll hold onto it.

And just like a child or a puppy or a plant that grows without us even noticing how big it's getting, our joy – our love of life – might just do the same.

So that one day we might not cling to the holidays and the weekends.

And one day we might look around and realise that we're not in the tunnel at all.

But that we are the light at the end of it.

WAITING FOR THE WEEKEND

They say we only live once.

But I don't think that's true. I think we only die once. We can't start over when we die. It's done. Final

But every morning is another chance to get up and live. Another 86,400 moments of living.

Too many of us are waiting on something before we start living. Waiting for the weekend. The summer. The new job. The weight-loss. Next year.

But why? We can live ourselves happy right now. Read a book, take a walk. Eat our favourite food. Live ourselves happy. Because I think that's the purpose of life – to live. Happily.

Every day we have 86,400 seconds,
moments,
chances
to live.

We only die once.

Let's die happy.

BOMB DISPOSAL

Sometimes [illegible]ions need diffusing.

Some peopl[illegible] try and do this from the outside, with loud voices and
heavy weap[illegible].
Like a battl[illegible]

And some [illegible] diffuse situations from the inside. Gently, carefully.
Like a bom[illegible]

There are [illegible] casualties in battle. It is messy, obvious. We can only
win in battl[illegible] others are lost.

But diffuse [illegible]omb and we can avoid bodies on the battlefield. And it
should alwa[illegible] be about avoiding bodies on the battlefield.
Diffuse a bo[illegible]b and no-one is lost.

Doing wha[illegible] right should always prioritise keeping people safe.
Wherever p[illegible]ble, it should not mean there are people left behind.

So if at all p[illegible]ible, don't start the battle.

Diffuse the [illegible].

HANDLE WITH CARE

Every woman I know has, at one point or another,
sobbed in the shower
cried in the car
swallowed down tears in the supermarket
and broken down in the bathroom.

And then she has dried her eyes, lifted her head, taken a deep breath and carried on.

She has walked into work
or in through the front door
or into the store or the coffee shop or the hair salon.
And she has smiled and chatted to people so that no one would know she had been crying.

And I'm not reminding us of this to say
"look how strong we are to pull ourselves together when we are falling apart". Although that still stands.

I'm reminding us how easy it is to paint on a brave face so that other people are none the wiser.

So whilst it might not have been you sitting in the car park crying this morning, it might have been that woman who sits three desks down from you.

Whilst it might not have been you sobbing in the shower before getting the kids ready for school this morning, it might have been their teacher. Or another parent on the school run.

Whilst you might have gotten round the supermarket without being on the verge of tears today, it might not be the same for the person working the till. Or the person behind you in the queue.

Everyone wears their brave face in public.

And we'll never really know just how many people around us have pulled themselves together with the thinnest of threads each morning. How many people are ready to fall apart again at any point.

But compassion strengthens those threads.

Compassion is powerful.
Because even when no one can see it,
even when no one can hear it...

They can feel it.

GOOD ENOUGH

We live in a world which tells us not to do things by halves. Where a job done well is a job well done and if you're not trying hard then you're not really trying.

It has made us feel as if we must be experts in everything. That we must commit for ever until we are at the very top of the game.

But here's what I say:

Learning to play the guitar and realising after three months that it isn't for you, does not mean you've failed. You have challenged yourself far more than if you'd never picked up the guitar at all.

Taking up running and quitting after five weeks because you hate every moment of it does not mean you've failed. You have moved your body more than if you'd never gone for a run at all.

The problem with having to give 100% is that it isn't sustainable. Sooner or later we run out of reserves – and then we end up giving nothing.

Fifty percent of something is better than one hundred percent of nothing. 'Good enough' sometimes really is good enough.

Every habit or hobby we adopt does not have to stay with us for life and we do not need to become experts at everything we ever try to do.

Picking something up doesn't mean we can never put it down again. We don't have to carry stuff forever.

Life is not a punishment. Allowing some things in life to be temporary does not mean we've failed. It means we are succeeding at being authentic, adaptable, content. Happy.

And surely 'happy' is not only 'good enough'...

But as good as it gets.

MEETING MOUNTAINS

Tomorrow is a new page. A new chapter. Possibly even a new book.

But remember that the only predictable thing about life is that it is unpredictable. There will be mountains written on to your pages that you hadn't anticipated or planned for.

People will tell you that they are there to be climbed. That you must scale them. That the view from the top will be worth every second.

But what if that's not quite what you're destined to do?

What if you're meant to move mountains? Or help someone to the bottom who got stranded on their climb?

What if you're meant to take the path around the mountain, not over it? What if there is something on that path that could lead you to your happy ever after?

Tomorrow is a new page. And so many people write loudly about the mountains they are going to climb. But remember...

Even at the bottom
There is still a stunning view
So when you meet a mountain
Simply do what's best for you

IN PLAIN SIGHT

Too many [illegible] are waiting around in the wings of life. Trying to blend into the ba[illegible]und or camouflage ourselves in the crowd.

Trying to [illegible]iet. Unnoticed. Invisible.

Because we [illegible]een made to feel that it's wrong to stand out unless it's [illegible] right reasons.

You can be [illegible]ut don't stand too tall otherwise people will notice you. Unless you' [illegible]upermodel. Then it's fine – go ahead, be tall.

You can ha[illegible]ur own individual style; but don't dress too differently otherwise p[illegible] will notice you.
Unless you [illegible] a designer clothing line from your individuality.
Then it's fi[illegible] ahead, be different.

You can be [illegible] at your job; but don't do too much otherwise people will notice [illegible]d feel inferior.
Unless you [illegible]ge to earn them all a bonus. Then it's fine – go ahead, work hard.

You can be [illegible]self; but not too much otherwise people will notice you.

Which doe[illegible] make sense.

Why should [illegible] you be noticed for being yourself?

And who d[illegible] which reasons were cause for fitting in or valid for standing ou[illegible]

We are shri[illegible] ourselves, trying to retreat into the background of our own lives.

Hiding in p[illegible] sight.

But we des[illegible] be ourselves. To be seen. Visible. Heard.

So hold you[illegible] up high and stand tall; even if it means you tower above the [illegible] Go ahead – be you.

Because if [illegible] going to notice you...
well then, [illegible],

you might a[illegible] give them something to notice.

GIRLFRIENDS

Platonic girl friend love is pretty special.

Watch how we sit at dinner, laughing so hard that our voices echo around the entire room and our smiles reach all the way up to our eyes as we reminisce about the moments that have bound us together.

Then watch how moments later one of us breaks down. Watch us pour out the things that are troubling us with such honest vulnerability that you can't quite believe it's happening at the same dinner table.

Watch us all reach out without thinking until there is a pile of hands in the middle of the table, silently saying "we are here".

Watch us cry at each other's graduations and weddings and when we meet each other's babies. Watch us feel each other's happiness so much that our bodies can't quite contain it.

Watch us take our children to the park and listen to us talk about how quickly they've grown and how fast the time flies.

Then hear how the conversation moves to tales of hardship and heartbreak so seamlessly that you barely even notice. Watch how we reach out instinctively to hug each other before returning to push our children on the swings, knowing we have been heard.

Watch a whole group of people be there for each. Be so comfortably themselves with each other that they can go from laughing to sobbing in a matter of minutes and feel nothing but loved, cared-for and comforted. Not embarrassed. Not judged. Just loved.

Because they know there will always be sunshine and storms in life. Ups and downs, highs and lows.

And they know there will always be someone there to celebrate the highs and to share the sunshine. But that there will also be someone nearby when it rains.

With space under their umbrella.

PHO[illegible]O FINISH

Check my r[illegible]ion in the mirror
Wishing I [illegible]ller, thinner
Wishing I [illegible] change the shape
Of everythi[illegible]hat's on my face

Wider eyes [illegible]hinner nose,
Skin that's [illegible]and smooth, that glows
Bigger lips [illegible]smaller face,
Thicker hai[illegible] perfect waves

Longer lash[illegible]blush applied
Cheekbone[illegible]pted and defined
Eyebrows [illegible], tighter grin,
Perfect mak[illegible]up, sharper chin

But now th[illegible]ure of perfection
Doesn't ma[illegible] my own reflection
Doesn't tell [illegible]real story,
Just a part [illegible] written for me

In the filter[illegible]he screen
In pages of [illegible]magazines
That show [illegible]ces with no flaws,
Without th[illegible]rinkles, lines and pores

And what b[illegible]d the filtered glow?
The parts a[illegible]ge cannot show,
Surely there[illegible]more to me
Than only [illegible] camera sees?

And yes, of [illegible]se, I know there is
It's taken ti[illegible] learn all this
But now it [illegible]'t pain to see
A picture
Where I lo[illegible]ike me

MAGPIES

She's the kind of girl who searches for another magpie when she spots only one.

The kind of woman who dances under ladders and tightrope-walks the cracks of the pavement.

The sort of person that uses a broken mirror to see her face from a different angle.

The type to befriend the black cat that's crossing her path.

She's the kind of girl that makes her own luck. Because she owns
her magic.
Her destiny.
Her fate.

Because she doesn't believe in one for sorrow.

She believes in living for joy.

THE MOTH

She always felt like a moth amongst the butterflies.

The plain and dull amongst the bright and the beautiful.

And as she watched them explore the big, wide world,
she wondered why she was always being drawn back to herself.
Why she seemed to be the thing she wanted and needed more than anything else.

And for the longest time, she couldn't understand.

Until
one day,
she realised.

She wasn't just the moth.

She was also the flame.

THE FIGHT

They'd heard she was a warrior.

And so they pictured her fresh from the fight –
with flowing hair and dirt etched on her face.
With fitted armour and a sword in her hand.

What they hadn't realised was that she looked like the woman stood next to them in the supermarket –
with messy hair and hurt etched on her face.
With creased jeans and a coffee in her hand.

Because she'd been fighting a battle they knew nothing about.
And even though it didn't look like much of a victory to them, it really was.

That she was there. She was fighting. She was strong.

And no matter what she, or the battle, or the victory looked like to anyone else,
the fact remained.

She was a warrior.

HUMAN BEING

I love my b[illegible].

This is such [illegible]bold statement isn't it?
Who admit[illegible] loving their body like that?

Well, I like [illegible] remember that love does not mean perfection.
It doesn't [illegible] flawless or unblemished or undamaged.

I love plent[illegible] people who are flawed and blemished and damaged.
I love them [illegible]cause of who they are. Of who I am when I'm around
them.

I love them [illegible]cause of what they bring to the world and what they bring
to my life.
And becaus[illegible] what I bring to life as a result of them.

So I love m[illegible]dy.

Some days [illegible] not particularly like it.

It may be h[illegible]ier, softer and more scarred than I would wish.
Some parts [illegible] not work as well as they used to.
But that do[illegible] not mean I do not have deep gratitude and love for
everything i[illegible] done and continues to do for me each day.

It works ha[illegible] me. It keeps me alive.
Sometimes [illegible]esn't do exactly what I want it to do.
It isn't as fa[illegible] as strong or as lean as I'd like.

But it does[illegible]eserve hate for that.

Just like th[illegible]le in my life do not deserve hate for the ways in which
they may n[illegible]eet my expectations,
and I do no[illegible]rve hate for the ways in which I may fall short of theirs.

I love my b[illegible].
It is not pe[illegible]. But nothing is.

Because we [illegible]ot here to be perfect, we are here to be human.
Here to liv[illegible]

And we nee[illegible] bodies for that.

So we migh[illegible]ell give them some love.

OKAY

Sometimes it takes nothing
And sometimes a little more
Sometimes just the smallest step
Will get you out the door

Sometimes it takes only
Just the tiniest breath in
Sometimes just a pause
And you are able to begin

But sometimes just that little step
Feels like a giant leap
And where that leap will take you
Feels too dizzying and steep

Sometimes that small breath
Feels like it's trapped inside your throat
As if you're underwater
And you cannot stay afloat

Sometimes when you pause
It's like you're rooted to the spot
Tied up in disquiet
With your stomach in a knot

Sometimes it takes nothing
And sometimes a little more
Sometimes life feels harder
Than the way it felt before

Yes, sometimes it takes all your strength
To go about your day
And sometimes it takes *everything*
To simply be okay

LIVING

Life in its [illegible] is breaths that we take
Our very [illegible]eath is just seconds away
And breath [illegible]sures we survive, we exist
But being [illegible] a lot more than this

It's climbin[illegible]ountain then looking back down
To see whe[illegible] started and where you are now
It's loving [illegible]w that you see from up there
With the [illegible] your feet and the wind in your hair

It’s meetin[illegible] friends to catch up over tea
And laughin[illegible]il you forget how to breathe
It’s dancin[illegible]ght ‘til your feet wind up sore
And singin[illegible] ‘til your throat feels raw

It’s walkin[illegible]each and it's watching the tide
It’s findin[illegible]ll to hear oceans inside
It's flying [illegible]can see clouds from above
It's countin[illegible] stars and it's falling in love

It's watchin[illegible] sun rise and watching it set
It’s gatherin[illegible]ments you'll never forget
The mome[illegible]at teeter and flutter between
A world ful[illegible]onder and one of routine

So breathe [illegible] out - it'll keep you alive
But know t[illegible]u're here to do more than survive
You’re here [illegible] music dance on through your veins
To climb t[illegible]op of the mountain again

To see your[illegible]y and to feel your heart leap
The world i[illegible]ow and you’ve got front row seats
So in the ne[illegible]onds, when you breathe on in
Remember [illegible]onder of life that’s within

‘Cause takin[illegible]reath keeps you living for sure
But the bre[illegible]aking moments?
They’re wh[illegible] live for

HEART SONG

Sometimes I hear a really old song on the radio, and I sing along automatically.

And I realise I know every word,
without thinking.

And it occurs to me that singing those words to myself all those years ago means that my brain can remember them,
recall them,
and feel them
at any given moment.

Because it has internalised those words without me even realising. So that it takes no effort to bring them to the forefront of my mind.

That's how powerful our brains are.

And it makes me think about the way we speak to ourselves.

See, if we'd learned to internalise not just song lyrics
but words that told us we were
beautiful
enough
and worthy
when we were younger, perhaps we'd be able to recall those words -
those thoughts, those feelings -
at any given moment too.

And maybe we'd have learned to believe them.

Believe that we are
beautiful
enough
worthy.

But it's not too late.

We learn the words to new songs all the time.

Maybe it's time to start singing from a new song sheet.

One that reminds us how absolutely incredible
and worthy
we really are.

FLA[illegible]ES

Striking a [illegible] too hard won't light it.
In fact, it [illegible] break it.
And then [illegible] will be no light.

Piling too [illegible] on a fire won't keep it lit.
In fact, it [illegible] suffocate it.
And then [illegible] will be no fire.

Burning a [illegible] constantly won't keep it burning.
In fact, it [illegible] aust it.
And then [illegible] will be no flame.

Sometimes [illegible] is better.
Sometimes [illegible] by little is needed.
Sometimes [illegible] is necessary.

Sometimes [illegible] ness gives us light
and space [illegible] the.

Sometimes [illegible] ness allows us to come back to life again when we
weren't [illegible] if we still had that fire in us.

So don't [illegible] hard on yourself.
Don't pile [illegible] pressure.
Don't burn [illegible] elf out.

Because [illegible] ne can't stay alive like that.

STAY WILD

It's ok if you've ever felt guilty or ashamed or angry. It's ok if you've ever felt scared or anxious or unsure.

Just as it's ok to have felt happy or brave or confident.

Because the world is wild.
And with wild comes both calm seas and crashing waves.
Still mountains and crushing avalanches.
Peaceful parks and forest fires.

Life is in parts glorious
and in parts a complete mess.
The world is polar opposites
and parallels all at once.

So it's ok to feel crushed.
It's ok to crash and burn.
It's ok to feel a fire rise inside of you
and also feel like you might drown sometimes.

Because that's life.

And noticing just how wild and messy it is
simply means you've looked around once in a while.

And decided
that it's still worth living.

TRADING PLACES

If one day [illegible] swapped places -
I was you [illegible] you were me
I wonder [illegible] is that both of us
Would act[illegible]e

I wonder if [illegible] notice
How your [illegible] lights up your face
How when [illegible] walk into a room
You bright[illegible] up the place

I wonder if [illegible] see the way
You always [illegible] the time
For those [illegible] seek you out because
You're pati[illegible]nd you're kind

And maybe [illegible]ould notice
How I alwa[illegible]nd my ground
And how I [illegible] those I love
When they [illegible]st or down

Perhaps I'd [illegible]ce how
I'm quite [illegible] all by myself
And how I'[illegible]ways there for others
When they [illegible]or help

And if you [illegible]our patience
And if you [illegible] see your smile
If I could h[illegible]yself
And feel my [illegible]ness for a while

Then mayb[illegible] would understand
We cannot [illegible]fined
By all that [illegible]ate on
In our min[illegible]nd our minds

Yes, if we both swapped places
And had someone else to be
Perhaps we'd come to realise
There's so much we cannot see

And maybe in the moments
You were me and I was you
We would see why people love us
And we'd learn to love us too

WAITING BY THE WINDOW

We waited nine months to meet you.
We waited to hold you, to watch you walk, to hear you talk.

And I'm not sure you realise this, but we now wait at the window every day for you to get home.
A home that is filled with all of your things, all of your noise.

But one day we will walk into your bedroom and there won't be clothes all over the floor.
There won't be snacks that you've abandoned in every room and there won't be the noise of some obscure TV show echoing through the house.

Yes, one day our nest will be empty.
Quiet.
Tidy.

You will not need us anymore like you do now.
And that will mean we have done our job.

It will mean we have succeeded
in helping you grow your wings and in teaching you to fly.

And we will enjoy the quiet and the tidiness,
knowing that this is how it is supposed to be.

But we will also miss you. We'll miss the noise and miss the mess that tells us you are here.

So I hope you'll know that you can fly back whenever you want to.
Need to. Wish to.

That you can call us and tell us to put the kettle on
and open the snacks because you'll be here soon.

Because I'm not sure you'll realise this, but we'll be here
waiting to watch you walk through the door. Waiting to hold you.
Waiting to hear you talk about what you've been up to.

Yes, even when you've flown the nest, we will be here.

Always.

Waiting by the window
for you to get home.

MATTER OF FACT

"I'm kind."
Are you really?

"I'm compassionate."
Are you truly?

"I'm gentle."
Are you actually?

Are you truly all those things with everyone that matters in your life?

I'm sure you would say yes. So I'll word it slightly differently.

Are you truly all of those things with everyone that matters in your life,
including yourself?

Do you speak kindly to yourself?
Do you treat yourself with compassion?
Are you gentle with yourself when life is tough?

Because I know you're all those things to everyone else.
You shower them with kindness,
grant them compassion
and you recognise when they need you to be gentle.

But you need those things too.
From yourself as much as anyone else.

Because I know you might have forgotten this...
but they're not the only ones that matter.

You matter too.

SUNDAY REST

Don't fall into the trap of thinking that
doing nothing is doing nothing
for you.

That being unproductive is unproductive
for you.

We've gotten so used to being busy,
so used to doing things with visible results,
so used to tracking our steps and logging our activity and ticking things off our to-do list,
that we've forgotten the importance of rest.

'Doing nothing' and being 'unproductive' are actually doing something productive.

They are helping you recharge.
Recoup.

Reading a magazine or having a bath or sitting in the garden with a cup of coffee are not a waste of time.

Time spent rested is not time wasted.

We are not machines.
We are not robots.
We are not here to
constantly work and move and do.

We are human beings.

And sometimes we just need to be.

SILVER LININGS

When the [illegible] waves engulf you
And there's [illegible] all around
And when [illegible] you're in so deep
You might [illegible] swim down

When the [illegible] looming darkly
And you can [illegible] your way through
When the [illegible] are overbearing
And they're [illegible] in on you

When every [illegible] is dangerous
And treach[illegible] to tread
And you de[illegible] stop
And stay fo[illegible] st instead

Well...

I hope the [illegible] sapphires
That buoy [illegible] with their blue
I hope they [illegible] a little
Of their pre[illegible] light on you

I hope the [illegible] prides itself
On all its [illegible] leaves
And helps [illegible] your brilliance
Through the [illegible] ness of the trees

I hope your [illegible] are gilded
And are line[illegible] golden hues
And ruby [illegible] grow through grass
That shines [illegible] diamond dew

I hope you [illegible] sunshine
And the wa[illegible] that it possesses
I hope you [illegible] way the clouds
Are shining [illegible] ir edges

'Cause there's richness in the darkness,
When you're lost, beneath the surface
There's treasure waiting for you
And I promise you it's worth it

So don't give up or in
'Cause pressure builds a precious stone
You've everything you need
And you are stronger than you know

So please keep going up and through
Keep walking, swimming, climbing
And keep on searching clouds for silver
Sewn into their linings

YOU

I think the best thing
someone can say to you is not necessarily
"you are beautiful, you are funny, you are generous" or anything like that.

No. I think the best thing someone can say to you is
"thank you for being you".

An acknowledgement that simply you being yourself
is something they are thankful for.

Because whilst your actions -
your beauty, your wit, your generosity -
might indeed be the reason for their thanks,
"thank you for being you"
says that you alone are enough.

More than enough.

That you alone are a blessing to them.
With no expectation going forward
to be beautiful or funny or generous.
Or anything else.

But to simply be you.
Yourself.

Knowing that you are not defined
by one wonderful thing you do.

But rather appreciated for the thousands of wonderful things
that you are.

BRICK WALLS

Not every p[illegible]ceived challenge we meet in life
is an obsta[illegible] must overcome.

When we h[illegible]umbling block
or a bump i[illegible]e road or a brick wall,
we are usua[illegible]ready
tired, exhau[illegible] and overwhelmed.

So maybe t[illegible]mbling block is not actually there to trip us up. Maybe
it's there to [illegible]on our fall. To give us somewhere to sit when we need
to catch ou[illegible]th for a while.

And perhap[illegible] bumps in the road are there to remind us to slow down.
When we h[illegible]een charging ahead too quickly and driving ourselves
into the gro[illegible]

And maybe [illegible]brick wall isn't meant to be scaled.
Maybe it's [illegible] there for us to lean against. To help us rest and regain
our strengt[illegible]d maybe when we're rested, we'll realise we can go
around the [illegible] or take it apart brick by brick.

Yes, not ev[illegible]stacle we meet in life is there to test us and teach us a
lesson.

Sometimes,
even when i[illegible]sn't feel like it,
some things [illegible]
are simply t[illegible] to help.

LOVE

I love listening to the rain pitter pattering on the hood of my coat.

I love watching storms dance around the sky from behind a window.

I love feeling the warmth of the sun when I'm sitting in the shade.

And I love hearing the waves crash against the rocks when I'm a mile away from the shore.

I love being reminded how the world lives so loudly, so proudly. That it crashes and falls and burns. And yet, it never fails to get back up and dance.

Yes, I love being reminded that the world is so completely, unapologetically alive.
As long as I'm sheltered and safe.

And I think that's how we should love others.

I think we should show them how spectacular it is to be alive. What it means to truly see and hear and feel and thrive in this world.

But we should also be their safe space.

So they know that,
if they fall,
if they crash and burn,
there's someone in their corner.

Helping them get back up
and dance.

LOO[illegible] AROUND

People in [illegible] pay no mind to the prince
Who was [illegible] from a frog with just kisses
And none [illegible] balk at the trees that can talk
And don't [illegible] that the stars can grant wishes

They think [illegible] ttle of speaking to mirrors
That answ[illegible] back from the wall
They sing [illegible] dryads and drink with the giants
Who tower [illegible] ndred feet tall

They do not [illegible] ne the fairies and dragons
'Cause those [illegible] s are already there
With captu[illegible] ncesses whose extra-long tresses
Mean peopl[illegible] climb up their hair

Yes, all of [illegible] eatures with fairy-tale features
Don't notic[illegible] nagic they make
So they over[illegible] half of what's in their book
'Cause it's [illegible] the plot every day

And mayb[illegible] are so blind to our view
'Cause it's [illegible] we know very well
And so we [illegible] op and don't listen to what
Kinds of st[illegible] r world has to tell

The stories [illegible] s as they're shedding their leaves
Just to wel[illegible] hem back come the spring
And the wa[illegible] stay – how we don't float away
From this [illegible] l of rock as it spins

The stories [illegible] s full of water and fires
With the p[illegible] flood and ignite
The mount[illegible] lcanoes, the rare double rainbows
The phases [illegible] n every night

And once [illegible], we would never have known
That we'd [illegible] explain it somehow
We'd have [illegible] led at more, we'd have stared with such awe
And perhap[illegible] hould do the same now

Because wi[illegible] eing and knowing, believing,
We'd say it[illegible] in a book
Yet there's [illegible] r abound in the world – all around
But we jus[illegible] rgetting to look

KINDNESS

"But it made you strong!"

How often we are tempted to say this to someone when they've been through a difficult time.

And it may well be the case.

But chances are that they are feeling anything but strong. They are likely feeling
exhausted
shattered
weak.

And they need someone who recognises that. Someone who - for just a while - can be the strong one for them. Can offer them a shoulder to cry on and an arm to support them.

Yes, when they feel like that, they need to rest.
They need to recharge, recoup and regain the strength they're being told they have inside of them.

Because what doesn't kill us makes us stronger. But it sometimes very nearly kills us -
exhausts us
shatters us
weakens us.

They didn't want to have to be strong.
They wanted life to be kinder.

And as it wasn't, it might help them more than we realise...

If we bring the kindness instead.

WONDERFUL

The most wonderful women in my life are the ones who have been there
at my least wonderful times.

The ones who held me when I cried,
helped me up when I fell
and held my hand when I was scared.

The ones who sat with me at rock bottom,
supported me to stand again
and held themselves up as a mirror
to remind me of my magic.

The ones who straightened my crown when it had been knocked out of place.
Who straightened it without me even realising.
Without pointing out that it even needed straightening.
Without expecting anything in return.

Yes, the most wonderful women in my life
are the ones who have continued to see my strength and my magic even
when I couldn't see it myself.

And I wonder if they know how incredible they are for holding me. For
helping me.

I wonder if they can see their own magic, their own strength.

And I wonder if they know...

Just how treasured -
just how wonderful -
they are.

SHADOWS

I think one of life's hardest but most freeing lessons is this:

Not everyone will like you.
And that's ok.

You don't have to like everyone you meet
and they don't have to like you.
That's how people work.

As long as you're kind and considerate,
whether other people like you or not rarely has much to do with you.

We tend to shy away from people who shine a light on the parts of ourselves we're unhappy or uncomfortable with.

People who walk with an air of confidence that we perceive as arrogance until we too have that level of self-assurance.

People we perceive as intimidating until we're strong enough to stand our ground and go after the things we want.

People we perceive as conceited until we realise the power that can be found in learning to love ourselves.

And until we learn to love ourselves, believe in ourselves and stand our ground, we will be uncomfortable around people who have already learned those lessons.

So if someone doesn't like you,
that's ok.
Stop blaming yourself.

You don't need to dim your light.

They simply need to search their shadows.

BLOOM

She is just li[illegible]sunshine
Brilliant ray[illegible] that warm the sky
But she is n[illegible] afraid
To let the r[illegible] fall from her eyes

She's happy [illegible]nding light and warmth
But knows [illegible]nd a doubt
That a life [illegible]always sunshine
Simply leav[illegible] the world in drought

And yet a li[illegible] always rain
Delivers flo[illegible] abound
And no one [illegible] to die of thirst
But no one [illegible] to drown

So she has [illegible] a balance
Though she [illegible]n't know she has
She's under[illegible] we can't be
Always hap[illegible] always sad

She simply [illegible] realised
This is why [illegible] come her way
She doesn't [illegible] that this is why
They're har[illegible] her bouquets

Yes, she is [illegible] oblivious
But seemin[illegible] they know
That she's j[illegible] the perfect person
To help all [illegible] flowers grow

SUNDAY BEST

Every morning I tell my children

"Do your best".

And by that, I don't mean I expect them to push themselves to their absolute limits day-in, day-out.

Some days our best will be filling every hour with high energy work. With pushing our mind or our body to out-perform what they have done before.

And some days the best we'll be capable of is getting out of bed. Of getting showered and dressed.

Some days, the best we can do is leave the house and take a much-needed walk outside.

Some days, our best will be to get through the day without breaking down or giving up.

Some days, our best will look to others like bare minimum.

But that's ok.

Your Monday best might look very different to your Sunday best and that's exactly how life is supposed to be lived.

You can't constantly out-perform yourself. Just because you're not moving upwards doesn't mean you're not moving forwards.

The only thing we should expect everyday is kindness.
Kindness to others.
Kindness to ourselves.

So, as you go about your day,
please remember...

Do your best.

Whatever that means
to you
today.

heART

If someone tells you they love a particular song or poem or book, go find it.

Listen to it. Read it. Purposefully.

Because that song or poem or book likely has the words to express,
to explain,
to communicate
what they have not been able to themselves.

That's why we fall in love with art.

Because of how it makes us feel.

But actually because of how it *allows* us to feel. How it can take the joy
or the heartache that we didn't realise was overwhelming us and hold it
up to the light for others to see.

So that others can recognise it too.
So they can join us in it or care for us in it.
So that we can realise we're never alone.

Yes, when someone tells you their favourite song or poem or book, go find it.

Go listen to it or read it
and you might just realise,

it allows you to feel something too.

STRONG

They asked me if she was strong.

And I said yes.
I said yes without hesitation.

Because I'd seen her pick her heavy heart up off the floor, even when it weighed a ton.

Because I'd watched her claw her way back from rock bottom, even when it was a steep and treacherous climb.

Because I'd seen her lift herself up and drag herself through life, even when she was tired and weary to her bones.

Because I'd watched her persevere, persist and press on even when she was carrying the weight of her world on her shoulders.

And they told me I'd misunderstood.
They meant how strong was she physically?
How much could she hold in her hands and carry in her arms?

But it was not me who had misunderstood true strength. It was them.

Because they hadn't realised that
all too often,
the heaviest things we hold
and the biggest weights we carry

are the things that can't be seen.

IMPRINTS

Imagine if we were all walking round with a magic pen.

And every time we made someone's heart happy, our name would be
signed across [illegible] as if it was registered there forevermore.

And it wouldn't matter if it had only been a moment of happiness -
a kind word,
a small gesture,
a friendly smile,
we'd still sign our name.

Well, we may not have a magic pen,
but we can sign people's hearts -
still make a little imprint, a little impact,
a little difference.

And the best thing about it,
is that we get what we give. That's how feelings work.

Angry people make others angry and hurt people hurt other people. And
it doesn't make them any less angry or hurt.

Only more [illegible]

So maybe...

If we give out happiness,
if we try to make others happy,
it will make us happy too.

If we give out love,
we'll receive love too.

And our hearts will be full of the names and the signatures and the
imprints of people just wanting to make the world a little bit happier and
a little bit better.

Even if just with a kind word or a friendly smile.

Even if just [illegible] moment.

JUGGLING

You have always caught the things
That life's been busy throwing
Thinking there would come an end
But it just keeps on going

Thinking there'd be less
But there is always more to bear
So now your only option
Is to keep it in the air -

To juggle it, despite the fact
It's getting rather heavy
To try to keep your balance
Though you feel a bit unsteady

And if you drop it all
You're going feel like you've messed up
When really, at the truth of it
You're holding far too much

See, it is not to you
To keep it always all aloft -
To keep the plates all spinning,
Stop the balls from being dropped

'Cause life can be a circus
But you're not a circus clown
And you cannot juggle everything
So put a few things down

UNCONDITIONAL

Self-love is a tough thing to conquer.
We love others far more freely, far my forgivingly than we love ourselves.

So let's think about it this way...

I bet if I asked you what annoyed you or frustrated you about your loved ones, you'd be able to tell me.

You'd talk about the way they leave dirty dishes in the sink or the way they never answer their phone because it's always on silent.

If I asked you to notice the way they looked, you might see their greying hairs or the fine lines on their face.

If I asked you to recall times they'd made a mistake, you'd probably be able to. Matter-of-factly, without judgement.

Because you love them.
And it's not love that is dependent on them having no wrinkles or being the perfect housemate.

It is just love.
And that's the power of it - it doesn't need perfection.

So grant yourself the same graces.
Stop waiting until you think you're perfect.
Nobody is.

Just think of all those imperfect people that you love so fiercely.

And then add yourself to the list.

ALIVE

I know there may have been times in your life when you've stopped dancing, stopped singing, stopped being yourself because someone was watching you. Judging you.

And you are not the only one to feel this way.

But I can't help thinking that we've got it all wrong.

We've been taught that we must only be ourselves if it suits other people.

We must only sing if it sounds pleasing to those listening.
We must only dance if it looks good to onlookers.

But we are so wrong.

The birds sing - not because we might listen –
but simply with the joy of being alive.

And the trees dance in the wind - not because it looks good for us –
but because they are alive. Living in the moment.
Whatever the moment may bring.

So sing as loud as you wish
and dance as much as you like.

You do not exist for the enjoyment of others.

You exist to be alive.

Properly, fully, beautifully alive.

ONCE

For years, I [illegible]d a certain mug for my morning cup of tea. One that someone bo[illegible] me as a present once.

They proba[illegible]rgot they'd even given it to me.

I once listen[illegible] a song on repeat for days because I fell in love with it after someo[illegible]ld me it was their favourite.

They proba[illegible]rgot they'd even told me that.

I once had [illegible]utfit that I wore over and over after someone stopped me in the stree[illegible]ompliment me on it.

They proba[illegible]rgot they'd even done that.

They proba[illegible]rgot.
But I didn't

I rememb[illegible] all, to the point where the mug and the song and the outfit bec[illegible]le things in my life that brought me great joy.

So never u[illegible]timate the little things you do every day. The seemingly trivial, forg[illegible]e things.

Because, w[illegible]hey might be trivial and forgettable to you, I can almost guarantee t[illegible]
for someon[illegible]se...

they could [illegible]irely
the opposit[illegible]

HEAVY

Carrying a bucket full of water takes more of your energy than carrying an empty one does.

A towel becomes heavier to hold when it's wet - and it also becomes useless.

Trying to swim in your clothes weighs you down far more than swimming in your swimsuit does.

The irony of holding on to things that are full of water is that
they drain you.
Exhaust you.

Because things are so much heavier when they hold water.

Things weigh you down so much more when they hold water.

Things are harder to bear when they hold water.

So let your tears go.
Cry until it feels like
every last drop
has been squeezed from your body.

Let go of some of the weight.
Some of the heaviness.
Some of the burden you bear.

And I promise you'll feel a little lighter.

CHASING TOMORROW

Today I wo [illegible] nd found myself
With less th [illegible] esterday
My life was [illegible] sing things
I had assum [illegible] re here to stay

Things that [illegible] seemed little
'Til they left [illegible] iant space,
Left an emp [illegible] ilence
And a longi [illegible] heir place

And I began [illegible] nderstand
That when [illegible] ame to shove
I longed for [illegible] I'd had
When I'd t [illegible] ght that was not enough

I'd always lo [illegible] ahead
Was always [illegible] ng more and more
Growing so [illegible] lacent
Of the thing [illegible] once wished for

Running to [illegible] orrow,
To the week [illegible] d, to next year
Forgetting I [illegible] ucky
For the thin [illegible] ready here

And all this [illegible] me realise
That my life [illegible] buy more time
So maybe I [illegible] spend my time
Loving this [illegible] of mine

And maybe [illegible] grateful
For the littl [illegible] ings I've got
That seem i [illegible] equential
But which m [illegible] an awful lot

So, tonight I'll thank the stars
Instead of asking them for more
And I will hope to wake with all
The things I've thanked them for

'Cause now I see that my todays
Are filled with time I've borrowed
And I shouldn't sit around and waste them
Chasing my tomorrows

GROWING OLD

AGEING

Ageing is not an affliction
It's not a disease we should cure
It isn't a fight or an enemy,
A battle we have to endure

It's not something we have to fight against
Despite what we might have been told
It's a gift that's denied to so many
Who would love to be here

Growing [illegible]

POWER

We are often wary of getting older.

We are conditioned to try and halt time
and reverse the signs of ageing.

And yet, whilst the ocean is billions of years old, it is no less powerful because of age.
It can still choose to carry you or drown you if it so wishes.

Whilst some trees have been growing for thousands of years, they are no less impressive than a ten year old tree.
In fact, they are more grounded and more rooted.
And with that comes incredible strength to weather any storm.

And whilst some mountains are millions of years old, they are no less formidable than those formed more recently.
They still stand tall and proud against a many billion-year-old sky.

So being old is not something to dread.
Ageing is not something that has to make us
weak and small.

It can be what makes us strong.
Formidable.

And powerful.

Yes, there is so much power in ageing.

So claim it,
harness it.

And above all...

Do not be afraid to use it.

CHANGES

Sometimes people tell us
"you've changed".

And I believe the best response to that is
"I hope so."

Because we are supposed to learn and experience things in life, and they
are supposed to help us grow. And growing means changing.

No-one tells a tree 'you've changed'
when its leaves start turning orange or its blossoms start to grow.

They take photographs of it.
They write poetry about it.
They paint pictures of it.

They celebrate its growth, and they document its changes.

Yes, when a tree changes, people do not question it.

They see its beauty
and they turn it into art.

TOO LATE

When we are young, we want to look older.

And when we are old, we want to look younger.

And there is a window in the middle of it all when we're supposed to look as we wish.

But we waste that time wishing
we were taller or thinner or curvier,
our hair was longer or shinier, curlier,
parts of our body were firmer and perkier
and we'd started to use anti-wrinkle cream earlier.

And by the time we realise we were perfect just as we were,
the window has closed. It is too late.

Too late to realise that all those things never really mattered in the first place.

But it's never too late to start letting go.
To stop wanting, stop wishing.

It's never too late to accept yourself.

To look in the mirror and realise that all along, you never needed to look older or younger or anything else.

You just needed to look like you.

DANCING INSIDE

"Life is not about waiting for the storm to pass.."

Except that sometimes it is. Sometimes you are waterlogged.
Weighed down and wading
through flooded waters.

And you are exhausted. Sometimes you've had too much of the storm.
Because sometimes it has taken too much from you.

So you don't have to dance in the rain you don't want to.
You don't have to embrace it if you think it might drown you.

You can sit and read a book. You can call a friend.
You can close your eyes and sleep.

Life isn't about waiting for the storm to pass. It's about figuring out the best way through it.

And sometimes that means facing it, sometimes embracing it.

And sometimes that means closing the curtains,
turning the music up,
and dancing inside instead.

EMBERS AND KEYS

When I am older, I might not remember
I might get confused and I might lose my temper
And there may be times when I don't know your name
Because it's been trapped, locked away in my brain

And though it will hurt to think I could forget you
Offer me smiles, hold my hand if I'll let you
And talk of adventures we had long ago,
Show me the photos of people I know

Play music we've danced to and songs we have sung
Read me the books I read when I was young
'Cause your voice and your words might just be the key
That opens the door – that unlocks it for me

And maybe the music will spark tiny embers
Of memories dormant and I will remember
Your name and your face and the words to our song,
The times and the places to which I've belonged

And it might last moments or minutes or more
As the fire sheds light through the crack in the door
But when the door closes and gone are the flames,
When you are once more a stranger again

Just know you'll have stirred something deep down inside,
Something familiar that I recognise
Something I feel that's not stored in my head
But right at the core of my heart space instead

Something that's stirred by your smiles and your stories,
The touch of your hand and the songs you sing for me
And though I'll have no words to tell you, just trust
That deep
        down
        inside

I'll remember I'm loved

I NOTICED

I remember sitting in a bar once and watching a woman dancing. She was so full of joy and life that I found it hard to take my eyes off her. She was mesmerising.

But I didn't [illegible] her.

I remember standing in the supermarket one day and seeing a woman who had matched her eye make-up to the colours in her headscarf. Her eyes shone when she smiled, and she looked radiant.

But I didn't [illegible] her.

I remember watching a fellow mum on the school run years ago. She had a toddler who kept stumbling, stopping to pick things up and pausing to point things out. And even though she was in a rush, the mum was so encouraging, so patient and so calm. I remember thinking what a wonderful parent she was.

But I didn't [illegible] her.

And how often have you probably been that person? Not the one noticing and saying nothing – but the one being noticed.

The one exuding calm, radiance and joy to such an extent that people will remember you years later as the person in the bar or the woman in the supermarket or the mum on the school run.

The one who was mesmerising. Wonderful.

And yet, you'll never know because they never told you.

But they noticed you. I promise.

CRACKS

I know you are tired.
I see it etched on your face in shadows and lines.

But I know that your fatigue goes far beyond your skin.

You feel it in your bones.

Your soul is so weary of this world. Of having to drag yourself through it when every moment feels exhausting.

And you think there is something wrong with you.

But I promise you,
there is not.

When water leaks from a bucket,
it is not because the water needs fixing.
It is because the bucket is broken.

You are tired
because the world that carries you is a little broken too.

And sometimes you are trying so hard not to step on the cracks,
trying so hard not to fall through them
that you have no energy left for anything else.

You are tired.
Your bones are weary and your soul exhausted.

But you do not need fixing.

You just need to learn to trust.
To trust that you can carry yourself.

So that one day, you might walk down the pavement
and pay no mind to the cracks in it.

Trusting yourself.

Knowing that, no matter what...

You are not going to fall.

UPS AND DOWNS

Where ligh[illegible]s, there's shadow
Where a ro[illegible]s, you'll find thorns
And where [illegible]dusk descends at night
The sun wi[illegible] at dawn

Where fear [illegible]s, there's courage
We are free [illegible] controlled
And where [illegible] exists a secret
There's a st[illegible] to be told

Each end's [illegible] beginning
Sometimes [illegible]veal the truth
And where [illegible] is growing old it's 'cause
At one tim[illegible] was youth

If you fail [illegible]edly
There's mo[illegible]nce you'll succeed
But the onl[illegible]antee in life
Is nothing's [illegible]anteed

'Cause life i[illegible]tradictory
Where less [illegible]en more
It's a parad[illegible] opposites
A constant [illegible]rd fall

In a world [illegible] silence deafens
And where [illegible] is icy heat
Where som[illegible]s things are awfully good
And someti[illegible]ttersweet

So when lif[illegible]ying up
Try not to l[illegible]get you down
'Cause som[illegible]s we must lose ourselves
To finally [illegible]und

And you ar[illegible] alone
So many ot[illegible]feel the same
'Cause the [illegible]onstant thing in life
Is that it's [illegible] to change

HOLDING ON

Loss is an inevitable part of life. And with it of course, comes grief.

Grief can feel like a deep, dark hole that we will never climb out of, but when it all feels hopeless, I like to remember that it works just like love.

Because, when we first fall in love, it is intense.
It is overwhelming and consuming and loud. We cannot think of anything else, and we constantly crave the one we love.

After a while it becomes less intense, but it grows.
It grows deeper, more comfortable. It settles down and settles in for the long haul, knowing that it is not fleeting or superficial. It is less consuming. Quieter. An undercurrent of our every day without overwhelming our every thought.

Sometimes something will happen to bring that overwhelming love back to the surface; moments of pride or surprise or nostalgia that remind us just how much we love someone. Moments where our love is once again intense and loud.

And then it settles back into our heart where it knows it will stay.

Grief is the same.

At first it is loud and consuming, intense and overwhelming.
We constantly crave the one we grieve.

Then it becomes less intense, less consuming. An undercurrent of our every day without overwhelming our every thought.

And sometimes something will happen to bring our grief bubbling right back to the surface. Moments where our grief is once again intense and loud.

And then it settles back into our heart where it knows it will stay.

Because great grief is born of great love.

So where grief remains, where grief rests,
it often helps to remember that love is there too.

Sitting with her arm around grief
and holding it tight.

AFT[illegible]LIFE

“In my ne[illegible]” said the tree
“I think I’ll [illegible] dragon,
Or maybe [illegible] mountain troll
Who owns [illegible] tavern

Perhaps I’ll [illegible] little girl
With secre[illegible]den powers
Or maybe [illegible] tiny ant
That lives a[illegible]st the flowers

Perhaps I’ll [illegible] a waterfall
Or burrow [illegible]ground,
Perhaps I’ll [illegible] a heart-shaped balloon
And float u[illegible] the clouds

Perhaps I’ll [illegible] a rocket
And I’ll fire [illegible]o space
Or maybe [illegible] a pirate
With a scar [illegible] his face”

“What do y[illegible]mean?” I asked the tree
And that is [illegible] he said
“You know [illegible] all die one day
But our sou[illegible]ill not be dead

So when th[illegible]ld assumes
That I have [illegible]ed eternal sleep
I’ll worry no[illegible]cause I’ll have
So much lif[illegible] in me

For they wi[illegible] my ever-reaching
Branches in [illegible] glory
And I’ll bec[illegible] the pages
Of a many-[illegible]ured story

And that is [illegible]ou’ll often
Find them [illegible]ing through the pages
Or turning [illegible]ew leaves
Of a tale th[illegible] known for ages

I will not look as I do now –
My life will be rewritten
But they will hear my echo
On the pages if they listen

So if you feel inclined to,
Take a walk into the woods
Take a bag upon your back
Packed with your favourite books

Then find a shady canopy,
A leafy spot to rest
And read the trees the stories
Of the lives they might live next”

LONELY

There is a difference between being lonely and being alone.

Loneliness starves you.
It steals your joy, and it leaves you empty.
It is dark and its silence is deafening.
It leaves you feeling stuck. Trapped.

Loneliness can turn you against yourself. It can whisper loudly in your ear and encourage you to become your own worst enemy.

But being alone – if you feel at peace with yourself – nourishes you.
Feeds you. It brings you joy and leaves you fulfilled.
It is calm and quiet.
It allows you to be completely yourself. Free.

Being alone allows you to know yourself. It lets you speak, and it encourages you to become your own best friend.

In both cases, you are on your own.

And the presence of others cannot completely eradicate loneliness.

But it can go a long way to bringing a little joy.
Shedding a little light.
Freeing you a little.

It can go a long way to feeding your soul and calming the silence.

And with the right company,
it can go a long way to reminding you to love yourself.
To find peace within yourself.

So that the next time you are on your own,
you might be alone.

But perhaps – hopefully –
you won't be quite so lonely.

COULD YOU?

One time I met a man
Who only had a month to live
And I asked him if he had
Any advice that he could give

He said "I wake each morning
Knowing I'm going to die
So each day [illegible] remind me
I am blessed to be alive

You see, my life's on countdown
As each hour's unfurled
I know the clock is ticking
On my time here in this world

But what you're overlooking
Is that it's the same for you -
You know that I am dying
But forget that you are too

So make the most of sunshine
And go dancing in the rain
And sing a little louder
When your favourite music plays

Notice nature's colours,
Savour everything you taste
Stop waiting for tomorrow
'Cause you've got no time to waste

And could you say convincingly
That you'd have no regrets?
If just the next few days or weeks
Were all that you had left?"

And then my breath caught quickly
When he turned to me and asked
"Could you say that you died happy
If this day had been your last?"

WALK BESIDE ME

Walk beside me Daddy
Hold my hand when I am small
Watch me as I'm learning
And please catch me as I fall

Sit beside me Daddy
And sing songs to make me smile
Teach me rhymes and lullabies
That you knew as a child

Walk beside me Daddy
When I'm nervous and I'm scared
Make me feel a little braver
Knowing you are there

Sit beside me Daddy
Read me stories, tell me tales
Where light drives out the darkness
And where good always prevails

Walk beside me Dad
And help to guide me as I go
Let me make my own mistakes
But teach me what you know

Sit beside me Dad
And let me know that I am heard
Let me know you'll always
Be my haven in this world

Walk beside me Dad
As I'm becoming who you made me
Through all the highs and lows
You must have been through as you raised me

Sit beside me Dad
And let us make each moment last
Let's look to the future
And speak fondly of the past

Because there'll come a day, I know
When our roles will reverse
And it will then be you who needs
To be held and be heard

So I will hold your hand Dad,
I will answer when you call
And I'll be there to steady you
And catch you if you fall

I'll sing the songs you taught me
As we sit and laugh together
And reminisce about
All of the good times we remember

And if life gets confusing
And you're vulnerable and scared
I'll be brave like you taught me
And I'll make sure I am there

And though the time will come
When you can no longer go on
And life will feel a little emptier
'Cause you'll be gone

I'll sit in peace for knowing
I hold so much love inside me
And even when you're gone,
I know that you'll still walk beside me

DESTINATION LIFE

People say that life is a rollercoaster.
Full of ups and downs. Highs and lows.

And I suppose that's right to some degree.

But what they don't tell you about, are the times when life is like a long train journey. No ups, no downs. Just life whizzing past the window without you even really noticing it.

They don't tell you about the times when it's a bumpy ride down a narrow lane where there's no escaping the potholes. Where it's just life showing you that sometimes things are in the way and you have to get through them.

They don't tell you about the times when it's a journey of twists and turns. Not highs and lows as such. Just life throwing curveballs that force you to keep changing direction.

They don't tell you that sometimes the train journey is a bit dull. That the bumpy ride has you clinging on for dear life or that the twisty, turny road has you feeling exhausted.

Life is a journey.
And not every moment can be exhilarating.

Sometimes we have to take the train in order to differentiate the highs and lows.

Sometimes we have to navigate the bumpy ride in order to appreciate the smooth sailing.

And sometimes we have to change direction in order to follow the path that's right for us.

All we can do is trust
that when the journey finally ends,
we're exactly where we're meant to be.

And that - for the most part -
we enjoyed the ride.

CHAPTERS

We all of us have chapters
That we wish we'd never written
Pages that we've torn or burned
Or locked away and hidden

We all have masks and costumes
That we wish we'd never worn
And lines that we have spoken
That we wish could be withdrawn

We all of us have characters
We'd strike clean from the page
And maybe big decisions
That we're desperate to change

And we are very tempted
To pretend they don't exist
To tell a perfect story
Where these things are all dismissed

But do not hide those chapters
They're your story's little scars
And they're crucial to your tale
Though you might not think they are

For without them all your story
Isn't quite the one you wrote
And we have to make mistakes
If we're to learn what matters most

Yes, without them all your story
Will be hard to comprehend
Remember - some things only make sense
When we're getting to the end

THE AUTHOR

Letters fro[illegible]ife is Becky's fourth collection. She has pre[illegible]usly published two rhyming collections [illegible]ne book of poems for times of grief and [illegible]s

Her favouri[illegible]olour is yellow (it was her inspiration [illegible]the poem True Colours) and her favourite season is Autumn (w[illegible]inspired the poem Letting Go). She is constantly inspired by [illegible]ure and the way it doesn't fight what comes naturally. She believes tha[illegible]mans could learn a lot from that.

When she's [illegible]t writing poetry, she is walking amongst the trees, marvelling a[illegible]e moon and reading light and fluffy romance novels (because so[illegible]things in life might not always have a happy ending but it does no har[illegible]o spend time in stories that do).

She can be [illegible]d hanging out at the places below (some more frequently than others [illegible] the easiest way to contact her is via email at info@becky[illegible]msley.com.

Facebook: f[illegible]ook.com/talkingtothewild
Instagram: [illegible]agram.com/beckyhemsleypoetry
TikTok: tik[illegible].com/@talkingtothewild
Pinterest: p[illegible]est.com/talkingtothewild
Etsy: etsy.c[illegible]/shop/talkingtothewild
X: twitter.c[illegible]/hemsleybecky
YouTube: y[illegible]ube.com/@beckyhemsleypoetry5560

Website: be[illegible]emsley.com

All links ca[illegible]ccessed by scanning the QR code

Made in United States
North Haven, CT
03 June 2024